SIGN LANGUAGE
LITERATURE SERIES

Raven & Water Monster

Illustrated by Kathy Kifer and Dahna Solar

Ane Rovetta
Story consultant

—

Published by:
Garlic Press
100 Hillview Lane #2
Eugene, OR 97408

ISBN 0-931993-82-2
Order Number GP-082

Introducing the **Sign Language Literature Series**

The **Sign Language Literature Series** presents stories from different cultures. Pacific Northwest native people from Alaska, British Columbia, Washington, and Oregon have their own variations of raven stories. In their stories, raven is often a force who changes or creates order, land forms, natural phenomena, habits, and customs. He is a hero, a trickster, a fool, a deceiver.

Raven and Water Monster is adapted from a Haida story. It serves to explain how raven gained his beautiful black color and how he brought water to the earth. The story is presented in simple language, full illustration, and complemented with illustrated signs.

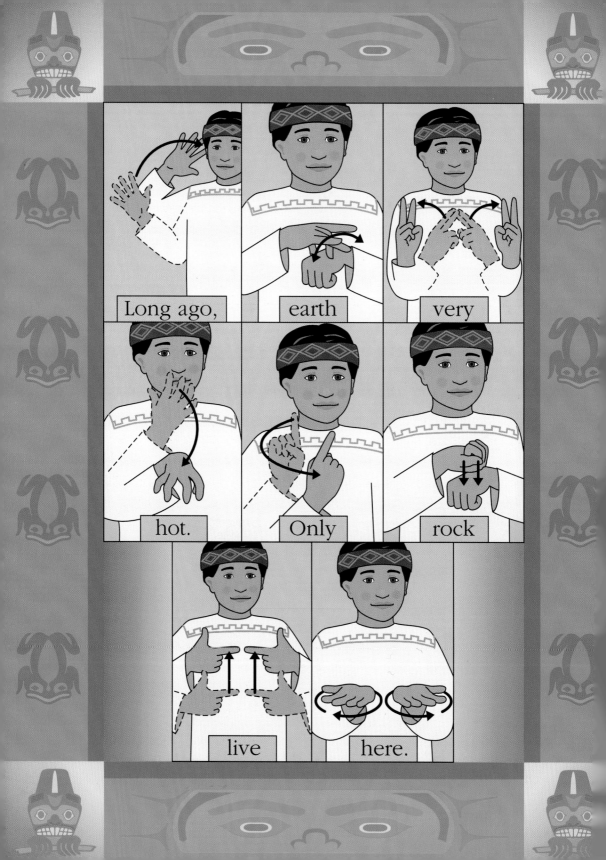

Long ago,   earth   very

hot.   Only   rock

live   here.

A long time ago, the earth was very hot.
Only rocks lived there.

 Raven

 white

 bird

 who

 want

 plant

 grow.

Raven was a white bird who
wanted plants to grow.

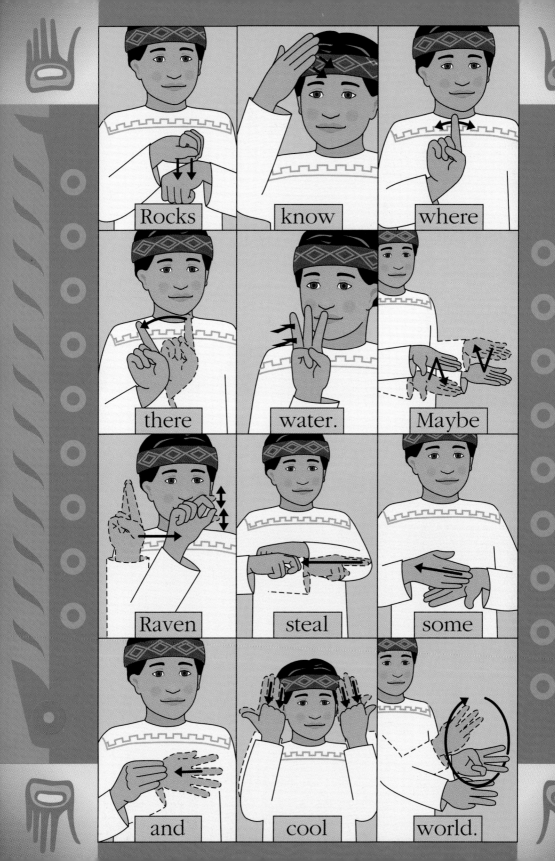

Rocks know where

there water. Maybe

Raven steal some

and cool world.

The rocks knew where there was water. Maybe
Raven could steal some and cool the world.

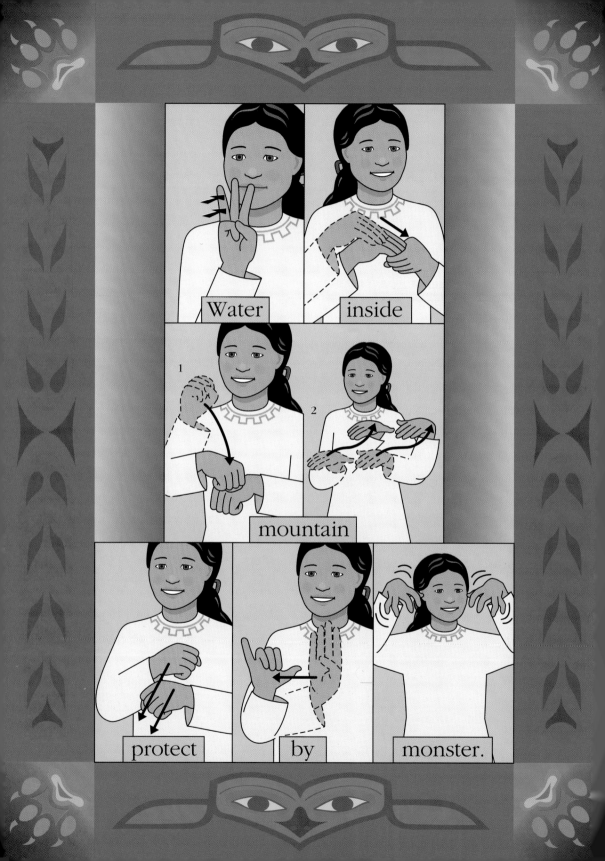

Water inside

mountain

protect by monster.

The water was inside a mountain
protected by a monster.

Raven

enter

mountain

tell

monster

story.

Raven entered the mountain
to tell the monster a story.

Story long boring.

Monster fall asleep.

The story was long and boring.
The monster fell asleep.

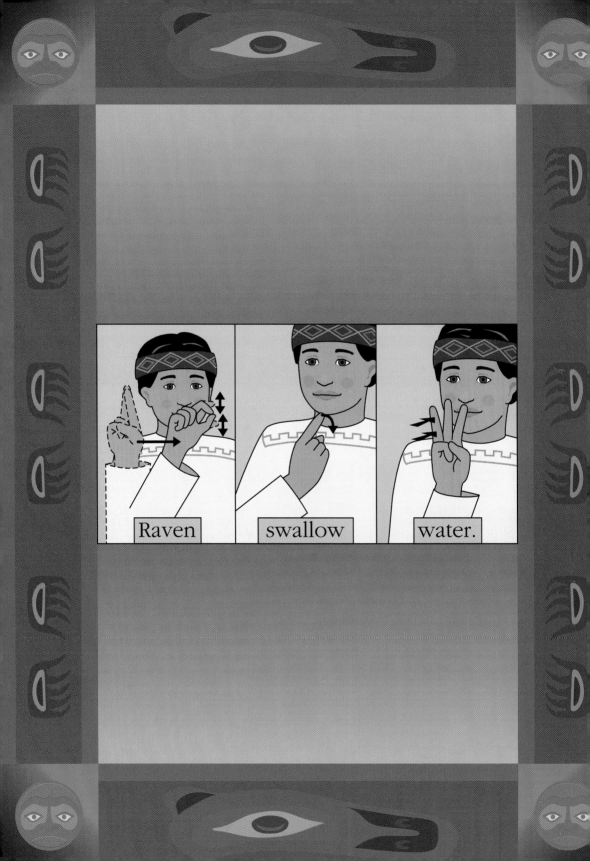

Raven   swallow   water.

Raven swallowed all the water.

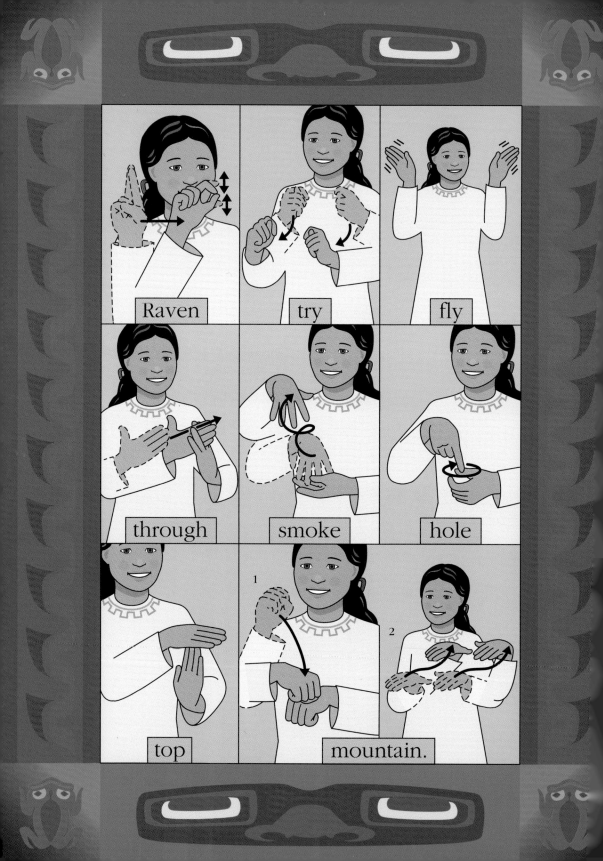

Raven tried to fly through a smoke hole
in the top of the mountain.

Raven   fly   up,

stick in   hole

awake   monster

Raven flew up, stuck in the hole,
and awakened the monster.

Monster angry. Make

fire under Raven.

The monster was angry.
It made a fire under Raven.

Raven   become

beautiful   black   bird

because   of   smoke.

Raven became a beautiful black bird
because of the smoke.

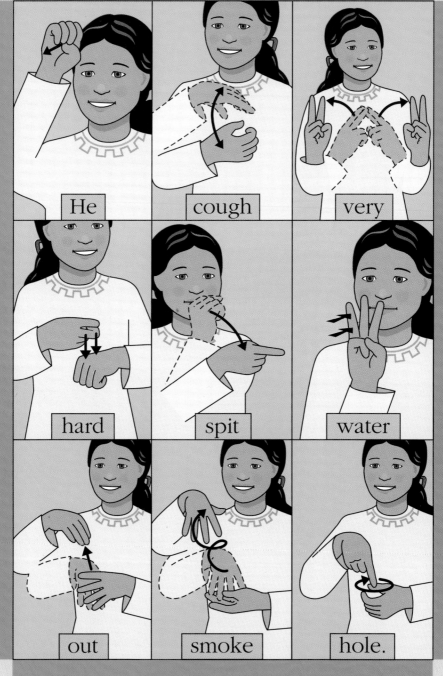

He   cough   very

hard   spit   water

out   smoke   hole.

He coughed very hard and
spit water out the smoke hole.

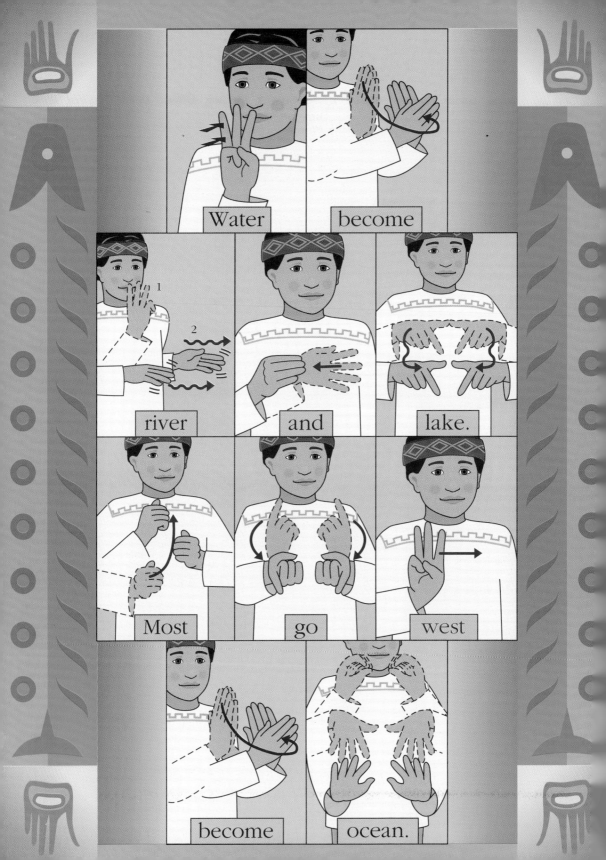

Water become

river and lake.

Most go west

become ocean.

The water became rivers and lakes.
Most went west to become the ocean.

Other sign language books from Garlic Press

Finger Alphabet GP-046
Uses word games and activities to teach the finger alphabet.

Signing in School GP-047
Presents signs needed in a school setting.

Can I Help?
Helping the Hearing Impaired in Emergency Situations GP-057
Signs, sentences, and information to help communicate with the hearing impaired .

Caring for Young Children
Signing for Day Care Providers and Sitters
GP-058
Signs for feelings, directions, activities, foods, bedtime, discipline, comfort-giving.

Mother Goose in Sign GP-066
Illustrated Mother Goose nursery rhymes.

An Alphabet of Animal Signs GP-065
Animal illustrations and associated signs for each letter of the alphabet.

Number and Letter Games GP-072
Presents a variety of games involving the finger alphabet, sign numbers, and recognizable, graphic signs.

Songs In Sign GP-071
Presents six songs in Signed English. The easy-to-follow illustrations enable you to sign along.